My Mommy Prayed For Me

Written by Donna S. Scott
Illustation by QBN Studios

Wow she's beautiful

Are you sure that's her?

God says she's My Mommy

She lives on Planet Earth

She's always on the go

But she always makes time to
pray for me

There's Mommy with Daddy

What fun times they have

I love to see them happy together

I giggle when I see them laugh

Come look at My Mommy
She went for a jog

My Mommy is so strong
She can do it all

Keep your smile Mommy

Please lift your head

I'm the twinkle in the night sky
That's what God says

Someday we'll be together

If only she could see me

My Mommy is so special

Until then I'll wait too

Today I saw Mommy

and to my surprise

She saw me too

I was there in her eyes

Dear Mommy,

I know waiting for me

sometimes you feel left behind

before you feel sad

please look around and you'll find

Waiting for me

is not what it seems

God is giving you time

To achieve your other dreams

There's Mommy with Daddy
They took time to rest
Seeing my parents happy
That's when I feel best

After all of our waiting

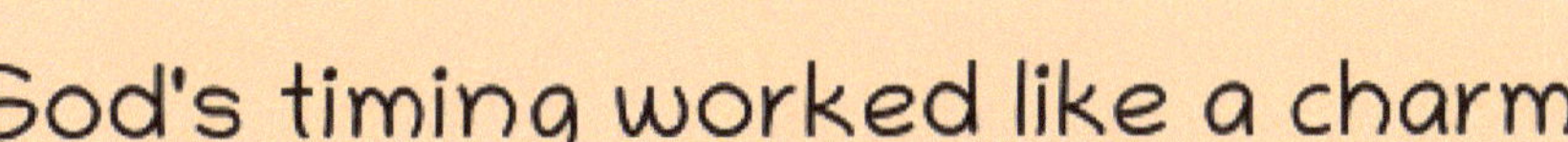

God's timing worked like a charm

I'm in mommy's tummy

The love from her heart is so warm

We waited so long
It seemed like forever

God says my mommy's
prayers and faith
brought our family together

Being here with my family is
something so great

My Mommy says this type of love
was definitely worth the wait

Love Worth the Wait

Author and Breast Cancer Survivor Donna S. Scott

Wrote "My Mommy Prayed for me" as a loving dedication to mothers in waiting.
The wait isn't always easy.
However, knowing that God aways has a plan for the future is a true testimony.

"I pray that this book is a source of encouragement and a friendly reminder that God has not forgotten about you and the promises he made to you."
Love Always, Your Friend Donna

www.ingramcontent.com/pod-product-compliance
Lightning Source LLC
LaVergne TN
LVHW070207110826
845147LV00002B/522